WITHDRAWN

The Open Sea

Kimberley Jane Pryor

Smart Apple Media

This edition first published in 2008 in the United States of America by Smart Apple Media.

Smart Apple Media
2140 Howard Drive West
North Mankato, Minnesota 56003

First published in 2007 by
MACMILLAN EDUCATION AUSTRALIA PTY LTD
627 Chapel Street, South Yarra, Australia 3141

Visit our Web site at www.macmillan.com.au or go directly to www.macmillanlibrary.com.au

Associated companies and representatives throughout the world.

Library of Congress Cataloging-in-Publication Data

Pryor, Kimberley Jane.
    The open sea / by Kimberley Jane Pryor.
    p. cm. — (Wonders of the sea)
    Includes index.
    ISBN 978-1-59920-142-9
    1. Marine ecology—Juvenile literature. I. Title.

    QH541.5.S3P786 2007
    577.7—dc22

                                                    2007004807

Edited by Erin Richards
Text and cover design by Christine Deering
Page layout by Domenic Lauricella
Photo research by Legend Images

Printed in U.S.

Acknowledgements
The author and the publisher are grateful to the following for permission to reproduce copyright material:

Cover photograph: Pod of dolphins courtesy of Alex Steffe/Lochman Transparencies.

age fotostock/Kelvin Aitken, p. 11; Doug Perrine/AUSCAPE, p. 24; Australian Fisheries Management Authority, p. 30; Coo-ee Picture Library, p. 23; Digital Vision, pp. 3, 5; Dreamstime, p. 6; Mike Johnson/earthwindow.com, p. 9; © Greenpeace/Grace 01/07/1993, p. 29; Robin Hughes, pp. 21, 27 (right), 28; Claus Qvist Jessen, p. 12 (top); Hans & Judy Beste/Lochman Transparencies, p. 13 (top); Eva Boogaard/Lochman Transparencies, pp. 10, 16, 25; Clay Bryce/Lochman Transparencies, pp. 14, 17; G. Saueracker/Lochman Transparencies, p. 15; Alex Steffe/Lochman Transparencies, pp. 1, 7, 18; NASA Goddard Space Flight Center, p. 4; NOAA/OAR/National Undersea Research Program (NURP), p. 12 (bottom); Photolibrary.com/OSF/Richard Herrmann, pp. 13 (bottom), 20, 22; Photolibrary.com/Pacific Stock/Doug Perrine, p. 19; Photolibrary.com/Peter Arnold Images Inc/Manfred Kage, p. 26; Photolibrary.com/Photo Researchers, Inc/Dr Paul Zahl, p. 8; Photolibrary.com/Phototake Inc/Roland Birke, p. 27 (left).

For Nick, Thomas and Ashley
– Kimberley Jane Pryor

J 3 4766 00333183 8

Contents

Glossary words

When a word is printed in **bold**, you can look up its meaning in the glossary on page 31.

The sea

The sea is a very large area of salty water.
It covers most of Earth's surface.

The blue part of Earth is the sea.

The sea has many different **habitats**. The open sea is a habitat that is a long way from land.

The sun warms the surface of the open sea.

The open sea

The open sea is the biggest and deepest part of the sea. It is so big that its end cannot be seen.

The open sea is a very large saltwater habitat.

The open sea is full of life. It provides food and shelter for many different plants and animals.

Huge manta rays swim in the open sea.

Plants

Large numbers of tiny plants float near the surface of the sea. In some places they grow so quickly that the surface of the sea turns green.

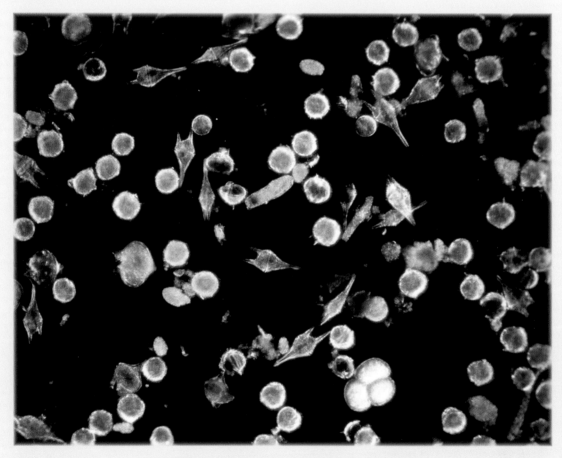

The plants that grow in the open sea are tiny.

During storms, seaweed is ripped from rocks near to **shore** and carried out to sea. If it floats, the seaweed becomes a home for young fish.

Young fish hide under floating seaweed.

Animals

Many different animals live in the open sea. In the daytime, sea snakes swim near the surface of the sea.

Sea snakes swim to the surface to breathe air.

At night, many animals travel to shallower water to feed. They return to deeper water when the sun rises in the morning.

Leatherback turtles swim in the open sea.

Where animals live

In the open sea, each kind of animal has a special place to live.

Flying fish live near the surface of the open sea.

Soft corals live on the sea floor.

A wandering albatross
glides above the waves
of the open sea.

Yellowfin tunas swim
in the sunlit water of
the open sea.

Survival

To survive in the open sea, animals need to find and eat food. Some animals use stinging tentacles to **paralyze** small fish that swim by.

The Portuguese man-of-war has hanging tentacles to help it find and catch food.

Gas-filled float to help it float on the surface

Stinging tentacles

Animals also need to protect themselves from **predators**. Some use their colors and others use their body parts.

Streamlined body for moving through the water easily

Powerful tail for swimming quickly

Mackerels can swim away from predators quickly.

Small animals

Many small animals live in the open sea. Most have clear, silver, or blue bodies. This helps them to blend in with the water.

Comb jellyfish are hard to see because they have clear bodies.

Some small animals live in very deep water. At night, they swim toward the surface to find food.

Squid swim up from the deep to hunt for fish at night.

Large animals

Large animals, such as dolphins and whales, hunt for food in the open sea.

Common dolphins often leap out of the water.

Sperm whales dive down into very deep water looking for giant squid to eat.

Sperm whales breathe in air at the surface before they dive.

Fish

Fish of all sizes live in the open sea. Most small fish swim in groups, called schools. Many large fish hunt alone.

The blue marlin is a large fish that hunts alone.

20

Most large fish can move with bursts of speed. They do this to escape from predators, and to chase and catch their own **prey**.

The Indo-Pacific sailfish is one of the fastest fish in the sea.

Some fish are very large. They are so big that not many animals attack them.

The ocean sunfish is one of the largest fish in the open sea.

Sharks are large fish that glide through the water in search of food. Some sharks swim into deeper water looking for octopuses to eat.

Blue sharks hunt in deep water for squid and octopuses.

Living together

Animals often live together for protection. Some fish form a spinning ball, called a bait ball, when they sense danger. The bait ball confuses their predators.

Dolphins try to scatter the bait ball to make the sardines easier to catch.

Sometimes animals survive by living with another kind of animal. Some young fish live under stinging jellyfish. The jellyfish protects them from predators.

Young fish hide among the stinging tentacles of a jellyfish.

Food chain

Living things depend on other living things for food. This is called a food chain.

This is how a food chain works.

Plant   food for

This is a simple open sea food chain.

food for

Tiny plants make their food using energy from the sun.

Plant-eating animal

food for

Animal-eating animal

food for

Tiny plants are food for tiny animals.

Tiny animals are food for whale sharks.

Threats to the open sea

The open sea can be **threatened** by natural events, such as very warm weather. Sometimes the sun heats the surface of the sea too much. Tiny plants do not grow well when the water is too warm.

Whale sharks need tiny plants and animals for food.

The open sea is also threatened by people who:
- put litter, oil, and **sewage** into the sea
- catch so many fish that some are in danger of becoming **extinct**
- drown sharks, dolphins, and turtles in fishing nets
- lose their fishing nets in the open sea

A hammerhead shark is trapped in a fishing net.

29

Protecting the open sea

We help protect the open sea when we:

- keep litter, oil, and sewage on the land
- stop catching **threatened fishes**
- use fishing nets other animals can escape from
- keep fishing nets from falling out of boats

Turtles can escape from some types of fishing nets.

Glossary

extinct   no longer existing

habitats   places where plants or animals naturally grow or live

paralyze   to make something unable to move

predators   animals that hunt, kill, and eat other animals

prey   animals that are killed and eaten by other animals

sewage   dirty water from homes and other buildings

shore   land along the edge of the sea

threatened   placed in danger

threatened fish   fish that are in danger of becoming extinct

Index